CW00693245

LITTLE BOOKS OF INSPIRATION

LOVE
LIVES HERE

Wisdom for a Happy Life

SUE THOMPSON

PURE
HEART
PUBLISHING

Sunsayer books may be ordered through Amazon.com
or by contacting:

www.sunsayer.com
hello@sunsayer.com

Cover and illustrations by Renée Lawrence
Edited and prepared for publication by Renée Lawrence

ISBN: 978-0-6456105-0-5 (paperback)
ISBN: 978-0-6456105-1-2 (ebook)

Reviews

"This book could not have come out at a more important time in our history. It is a potent reminder of the love that is present in all of us, all the time, under all circumstances, and the power of allowing this innate love to flow — a power filled with peace and harmony that starts from within and then spreads out into the world. This love can change the world."

— ***Christina Zampas,***
international human rights lawyer, Switzerland

"I find this book to be a wonderful way to set the tone and intention for my day or as a way to relax into my meditation. Realising and settling into my true nature takes time and needs daily reminders, and this book is a great tool to help me do just that."

— ***Ben Steen,*** *founder,*
Monkeymind Solutions, Belgium

"What a gift to the world: profound and yet simple messages from deep within. Bathe in it! Let it have you! Let yourself be transformed by it! Let love speak to you!"

— ***Dr. Clivia von Dewitz,***
Youth Court judge, Germany

"If you haven't yet discovered Sue Thompson's work, this is your lucky day. The knowledge she brings forth can change your world."

— ***Susan McKendry,*** *chairperson,*
Conscious Ground, Australia

"So beautiful, so rich and endearing."

— ***Eddie Ngatai,*** *founder,*
Mauri Tau Unfolding, New Zealand

Little Books of Inspiration

The Little Books of Inspiration series shares uplifting snippets of wisdom to remind us all of what is truly important and guide us toward deep states of happiness and love.

The series is intended to inspire reflection and self-discovery no matter which book in the series you are reading. Open any page any day and you'll find your heart's pure intelligence has led you to what you need in that moment.

We share with you the most poignant extracts drawn from thousands of hours in dialogue with Universal Wisdom* on topics that open the hearts and minds of those seeking to know themselves and others through a lens of love and possibility.

We are so privileged to have access to extraordinary perspective to support our awakening and demonstrate how to navigate these incredible times of change.

Our Little Books of Inspiration are stepping-stones on the path to freedom.

*Just like a modem connects to the Internet, Sue is able to receive high frequencies of intelligent, loving energy from what is often described as the Angelic Realm, Ascended Masters, the Unified Field, or Source. Call it what you will, we call it Universal Wisdom.

About the Little Books
of Inspiration Team

The Little Books of Inspiration Series is a collaboration between Sue Thompson, Renée Lawrence and Universal Wisdom. *LOVE Lives Here* is the first in the series that we hope will inspire you to live immersed in happiness.

For many years now Sue has been receiving Universal Wisdom through a process of relaxing her egoic awareness and opening to expanded states of consciousness, accessing loving guidance always for the purpose of broadening perspective and deepening the understanding of life itself.

The infinite source of wisdom has become our foundational offerings, shared with the desire to inspire self-awareness, enable people to access their own intuitive intelligence and live truly enjoyable lives.

Renée Lawrence artistically curates the wisdom to create the Little Books of Inspiration. Renée's profound capability to structure, edit, illustrate, and display the work is what makes the Little Books of Inspiration possible.

Together we invite you into our world of love and inspiration.

For Teo and Mokoan
May you always know the
love you bring to our world

Introduction

What is love?

For so many years, I thought love was all about other people. So much of what we see and hear tells us that. We grow up believing that love comes to us from others, and we share love with others. And, of course, this is true.

Yet there is an experience of love that is not promoted or often recognised. It is the most valuable gift of life. When felt and embraced, it offers so much and demands very little. So simple and available at any time. No one on the planet need go without love, even if they are alone.

This love that I speak of needs no Valentine, hearts or greeting cards. This love knows you in ways others never will. This love never criticises or expects more from you than you can offer. It has no conditions nor limits itself in any way. No boundaries are required. It demands no special behavior or generosity. Never is it jealous or competitive.

It always wants what is best for you and is constantly encouraging you to grow beyond what you might think you are. It sees ahead and lights your path. It smiles in the darkness and opens your heart.

This love that I speak of is here for you, always *and* in all ways. It is not known with words. It springs up from within and connects you with others in beautiful ways. It is *your love*. It is the essence of *you*. The energy of life that you are is the energy of love, pure and untainted.

When the feeling of love within you is unhindered by the chatter of the mind, you know there is more of yourself to discover, more to feel, experience, and express. Once felt, freedom is known.

The wonderful feeling of being "in" love, without any reason or reflection, reminds you of how precious you are. It encourages you to value the one thing you can't live without. You.

As you begin to explore this feeling of love within yourself, for yourself, of yourself, your thirst for life grows. Your sense of self-worth and value expands, and your courage to go beyond the limiting idea of yourself is awakened.

When this feeling of love takes over, your desire to share it with others is unquenchable. There is nothing you need in return, for you are already experiencing everything love is, and yet the reflection of pure love in the eyes of another enhances the joy of life.

In these pages you'll find simple statements to bring your attention to the most important thing in life: *your experience of the life you are living.*

Alive in the feeling of love, you create your future.

The Wisdom
Begins

Love is your greatest gift to yourself and others.

There is no richer feeling
than the experience
of this energy
we call love.
The feeling of love
within you is priceless.

There is no romance
you could ever have
that is as rich and fulfilling
as the love of yourself.
Enjoy the deepest embrace
of this connected feeling
of love as life in you.

When we look
for another
to provide love,
we are really looking
for someone to spark
the memory of love
within ourselves.

Only you can offer yourself the experience of love.

Love

is always

within you.

ALWAYS.

Fill yourself
with the awareness
of love, and from
that place you are
so potent in all
that you do.

You have heard the adage
"love conquers all."
It is completely useless
as words yet extraordinarily
powerful as the experience.

The presence
of love can melt
a heart of stone.

When you feel
full of love,
it is uncontainable.
You just want
to share it!

This is the richest
medicine your body
could ever require:
saturating yourself
in the experience
of love
in this moment.

Be generous
with the light
and the love
that you are.

You will find that your
relationships are
far more enjoyable
and pure when you are
overflowing with love.

When you are in
the presence of love,
you cannot be in
the presence of fear.

In every moment
you have access
to the most potent energy
in the world,

LOVE.

As you increase
your experience of love,
compassion and gratitude,
you expand your awareness
and your ability to sense into
the true wisdom
of any situation
you find yourself in.

Give yourself the gift of love.

It is the fuel
that will take you further,
will allow you to see more,
to experience more,
and most importantly,
to share the best of yourself.

The energy of love is your natural state of being.

People
who are awakened
to their natural state
of consciousness —
seated in love,
making decisions through love,
present in love —
not only have a better time
but show others that even
amongst all of this mess,
the most powerful way through
is with love.

When you open to the experience of love, you are accessing your infinite intelligence, and that's where the insight comes from, the wisdom, the ability to navigate situations from that calm, deep, relaxed place within. This is truly powerful.

The energy of life that you are —
love — is so much more powerful
than the physical and mental idea
of yourself, so much more intelligent,
so wise and wonderful. When you
are present in this energetic state,
you are connected to everything.

The more you allow yourself
to feel and sense life and love
within you, the more radiant
and whole you are.

You are a gift
to the world.

When you base yourself
in the energy of love,
you have access to the
greatest, most potent,
powerful energy
in existence.

The very core of what
you are is the inseparable
blend of love, light,
and intelligence.

Start every day with love.

End every day with love.

The energy of radiance is love.

When you know yourself
as intelligent love and light,
you can bask in life as if
your nearest and dearest
are holding you in the most
beautiful caress, as if you are
being held by God,
knowing there is nothing
that you could do or have done
that would diminish
this expression
of love within you.

If you are denying yourself love,
appreciation or self-recognition,
you are dimming your light —
holding back on the possibilities
and the potentiality that you are.

Fill yourself up
frequently with love,
with self-encouragement
and feel yourself bursting out
of your body as your radiance
pours forth.

When you set the intention
to increase the balance of love,
you notice the effect.
When you do it collectively,
you amplify that effect.

Magnificence

= love

magnified!

Miraculous things occur
when you come
from this place
of magnified love.

Being in love is not a story.
It is not a romance.
It's an experience
of energy in a moment.

Those who express without love find the expression energetically expensive. Those who express full of love find their expression effervescent.

When you give something love
and open your heart
to receive in the same instance,
you are in the moment

as love.

You always have the potential
to experience the energy of love
within your story,
within your circumstances,
within your body,
deep within your being.

Every time you express love
and joy, every time you hold
compassion for another,
every time you resist negativity
and nastiness, you are bringing
so much more love to the world.

The most powerful commonality of life

is love.

We promise you the best
Christmas present
you will ever unpack
is self-love,
loving the feeling
of life within,
for it is the fuel
of your life.

Feel the deliciousness
of just being immersed in love
for a moment
— no story, no name, no vocation —
just the energy of you.

Love and self-appreciation
are the fastest ways
to reconnect with that
magnificent life force
that you are.

When you send a radiant impulse of harmony out into your world, you are contributing to your own well-being and that of the collective consciousness.

Be in the feeling
of LOVE first.
Then go about
your day.

Attend more
to the experience
of love within yourself,
for this is
the energy of life.

The greatest experience of love
possible to any human being
is the fullness
of knowing yourself.

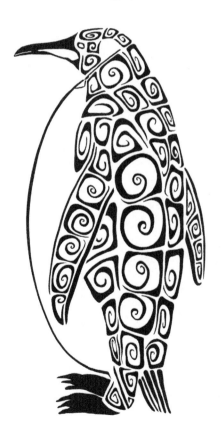

Love lives here,
right here
in your being.

Being connected to your
full source of love
is the best high
you could ever experience
in physical form.

The most important thing
is to immerse
yourself in love.
Love, light and laughter.

When you are
full of love
you can't find fear.

Your body is simply
the container
of love and life.

When you bring your attention back
to your heart and feel the sense
of powerful, loving energy within,
you are amplifying this whole field
of love that is universal,
that we are all part of.

One of the most devastating,
painful and toxic experiences
of withholding love and
forgiveness from another is
that you poison your own heart,
for you maintain a story
of separateness and pain.

When you are trying
to heal or help others,
simply bring them back
to the present moment
and LOVE.

Feel the worthiness of love within.

Be immersed in love as yourself
and bring that love to your world.
Let everyone feed off
the love that you bring.
Rich, beautiful,
better than chocolate!

You choose love
for yourself, here
in this moment!

In whatever way fear shows up,
know those structures
of fear are established
to defend, attack or paralyse.
When these structures
are set in the foundation of love
they are established to create.

As you refuel in the state
of loving relaxation,
you will find inspiration,
insight that embraces
foresight, and you are able
to look at your world from
a different perspective.

Teach children to always
come back to love,
to find their sense
of self within.

Love

is

contagious.

Breathe

love

deeply!

Love is that creative energy that sits within you ALWAYS.

Tap in and
love the feeling
of your presence.

Be this experience

of love

within yourself.

Whenever you find yourself
gravitating towards fear,
whether it be a collective
dialogue or your internal voice,
come home to love,
open to love,
and fill yourself up.
Once you are full and whole
you have access to the wisdom
you need.

The experience
of peace is love within,
still, settled, complete.
So when you feel peace,
you are in a state of love.

Love is not just a word.
It is a vibration,
it is a feeling,
it's energy.

Know yourself
completely and you
will deeply know love.

What you eat and how you take care of yourself are important, yet the most important fuel of life is love.

You are in a position
to offer an alternative
perspective from a place
of love, from a place
of possibility, not fear
or defence.

Can you imagine a world
where a large proportion
of the population is tuned into
their own powerful love,
where everything organises
around the frequency
of love, light and possibility?
Immediately you have
a different world!

When you come into
a state of presence, you will
find a well, a very deep well
of love and wisdom.
When you immerse yourself
in that well,
you will discover all is well.

The best decisions are made from a place of peace and love.

Allow yourself
this unlimited love,
feeling it for no other
reason than
the experience
of love itself.

Bring
your presence,
your curiosity,
your love,
your warmth
to any conversation,
and you will be unlocking hearts
everywhere, even those
you least expect to.

When you choose
to illuminate your day,
to light up your circumstances,
you are deciding to show up
from love, from light,
from radiance,
knowing that you are part
of a big, transformative
ecosystem.

The most important thing
in life is to begin
to experience
self-appreciation,
loving the energy of life
within you.

Try saying to yourself
in the morning:
"Can I allow myself more? Yes!"
And "LOVE lives here!"

Live well, live light, live LOVE.

The more of your spacious self
you discover,
the more you will recognise
that you are intelligent energy,
and it feels like love.

If you are
withholding
love from yourself,
you are withholding
yourself from life.

The more love you throw
at transformation,
the more you amplify
your own potency.

When you become seated
in love, unfolding within
your presence, you will find
that you can navigate

anything.

If you are feeling aligned
with love in the midst
of turmoil, you know
that you are aligned
with what has been divined
for you by you.

What a gift when
you are so full of love,
so full of energy,
so full of your natural
being of life that you have
more to offer others.

This is a time
for higher intelligence.
This is a time
for the power of love.
This is an age of light.
Be your light.

Put your weapons down
and let love speak.

Imagine the impact of love
in the world
if we were all being
a beam of love.
What would be possible?

Allow LOVE more space!

When you are connected
to love, you amplify
your energy, and all
of your life experiences
begin to flow.

The best, the juiciest,
the most delicious
relationship
you will ever have
is with yourself.

Being in the company
of things without ego,
such as nature and animals,
is a fast way to connect
with the energy of love.

When you immerse
yourself in self-love, you
immerse yourself in awareness,
in the sensation of the life
that you are.

When you are in deep relationship
with yourself, you are not needing
anyone else to value you
for you know your value within.

When you go to your heart
you will notice there is
no question there, only love,
compassion and intelligence.

Immerse yourself
in the magnificence of who you are.
Love that deeply
and invite another
into your experience.

You are here.

Life is here.

Love is here.

It's always here.

LOVE
lives
HERE,
in YOU!

Gratitude

If this book resonated with you we'd love to hear about it on our Amazon book page. Honest reviews help people find the right book for them.

Thank you for reading *LOVE Lives Here*. We hope you have felt the sparks of love within you that become the burning flame that lights up your life. Should you wish to explore deepening this love with our support, join us at sunsayer.com.

Next in the
LITTLE BOOKS OF INSPIRATION SERIES:
Freedom From FEAR
The Grace of GRATITUDE
My PEACEFUL Place

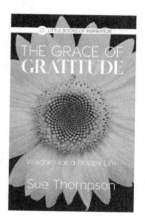

We would love to support your journey through our many offerings. To join our tribe of evolving people and be informed of new releases, head to sunsayer.com.

About the Author

Sue Thompson

Sue Thompson was born in Sydney, Australia, and now lives with her husband, Grant, in beautiful New Zealand. Surrounded by the purity of nature, she has developed the ability to access expanded states of consciousness and directly receive the loving wisdom and intelligence the Universe has to offer. This wisdom has enhanced her life in extraordinary ways, and she is blessed to love and be loved by a beautiful family.

Printed in Great Britain
by Amazon